RHYTHM OF LIFE AND DREAMS

INSPIRING INDIAN POETS

RAJESH PANAYANTHATTA

Made with ♥ on the Notion Press Platform
www.notionpress.com

Dedication

At the Feet of Poets who passed away after enriching the Indian Poetry

ꕥ

Contents

Contents

About The Author

Rajesh Panayanthatta, an Advocate on Record in the Supreme Court of India, was born in Kannur District of Kerala as son of Late Shri. K.K. Raghavan Nair and Late Panayanthatta Sarojini Amma. From childhood onwards his interest in poetry blossomed into a passion and he began writing poems, most of them in Malayalam language.

In 1993, he entered the mainstream of poetry publishing with a poem, "Theyyam" in the Balapamkthi of Mathrubhumi Weekly, a leading literature periodical in Malayalam. He has been publishing various poems in mainstream magazines, periodicals, journals and also in digital platforms.

Other Published Books:

- Manikarnika (Collection of poems) published by Forrest Books
- Kalindiyorathe Neelakkadambukal (Collection of poems) published by Olive Books

Awards:

- Thanal Award from Kozhikod Theemarathanal Sahithyavedi
- N.V Bhaskaran Memorial Special Juri Award from Kodungallur Kavyamandlam
- Pradeep Meenadathusseri Award from Parasparam Magazine, Kottayam
- Saparya Ramayana Kavitha Special Juri Award

Wife: Minu, **Children:** Revathi, Tapanya

Address:

Flat No.503, Tower No.22, Paras Tierea,
Noida Sector – 137, PIN - 201305 (UP),
Mob:- 9891549409
Email: rpanayanthatta@gmail.com

Preface

For generations, Indians have celebrated an ancient tradition of poetry. Poetry has always been an integral part of Indian culture and literature, with a rich history spanning thousands of years. From the Vedic hymns and epics to the works of contemporary poets, Indian poetry has evolved over the centuries.

This book is an attempt to honor the poets who lived in different parts of India in different eras. It is not a comprehensive study or biography of the poets, but rather a tribute to their contributions to the Indian poetic tradition. The poets featured in this collection were chosen without any particular formula, but rather as a reflection of the writer's admiration for their work.

These poets come from different parts of India, bringing with them their distinct cultural and linguistic backgrounds. Through their poems, they reflect on the complexities and nuances of Indian society, exploring issues of gender, caste, identity, and more. They also offer a window into the universal human experience, delving into themes of love, loss, longing, and the search for meaning and purpose.

Indian poetry has travelled through various styles, including Devotionalism, Romanticism, Realism, Impressionism, Expressionism etc. The works of these poets have had a profound impact on Indian literature and society, inspiring generations of readers and writers. They have challenged conventions, questioned norms, and provided a voice to the marginalized and oppressed. Their works have also been translated into multiple languages, making them accessible to a wider audience and further cementing their place in Indian literary canon.

This book is only a small attempt to introduce readers to the diverse and vibrant world of Indian poetry and to inspire them to engage with the works of these remarkable poets. It is a celebration of the power of words and the enduring legacy of Indian poetry.

With Lots of Love,

Adv Rajesh Panayanthatta

I

Mahakavi Kalidasa - The Master of Indian Poetry

"Oh mighty cloud capable of carrying immense
quantities of water;
Oh noble relative of Pushkara
Please take a message from me to my wife!
She lives in my house in Alaka,
The kingdom of the Lord of Wealth, Kubera."

The above lines quoted from"Meghadootam" a celebrated poem of Mahakavi Kalidasa, which is a work that touched the sky of Kalidasa's poetic talent. In what manner should Kalaidas's poetic skill be praised, especially for selecting an inanimate cloud as the messenger for his dearest? No doubt, Kalidasa is a Venus star in the poetic tradition of India. No matter how many stars shine in the sky, there are few stars that shine with the brilliance of Kalidasa.

Kalidasa is hailed as one of the greatest poets of all time, and is widely recognized as the master of Sanskrit poetry. Born in ancient India, his works have stood the test of time and continue to inspire and captivate audiences of all generations. Kalidasa's writing is renowned for its elegance, simplicity, and depth of meaning. He was one of the nine gems of the Palace of King Vikramaditya, an ancient Ruler in India.

He wrote two Mahakavyas i.e 'Kumara Sambhava' and 'Raghuvansa'. His other famous works include the 'Abhijnana Sakuntalam' (The Recognition of Sakuntala), 'Raghuvamsa' (The Lineage of Raghu), and 'Syamala Dandakam' (Description of the beauty of goddess Matangi). These works are classic examples of his skilful use of imagery, metaphor, and masteries in language.

'Abhijnanasakuntalam' is a play that tells the story of Sakuntala, a young woman who lives in the forest with her father who fell in love with King Dushyanta. It is a tale of love, separation, and eventual recognition that is both heart-warming and tragic. Kalidasa's use of language and symbolism is masterful, and the play continues to be performed and studied by scholars today.

In ‘Raghuvamsa’, Kalidasa paints a vivid portrait of the heroic Raghu dynasty, tracing the lineage of the great king Dilipa down to the illustrious King Rama. The poem is filled with tales of valor, honor, and sacrifice, and is a tribute to the great Indian tradition of martial glory.

"Malavikagnimitram" is a play that tells the story of the love between King Agnimitra and the beautiful Malavika. This work is notable for its portrayal of women as strong and independent, a rarity in ancient Indian literature.

Kalidasa’s poetry is known for its lyrical and romantic nature. He is famous for his ability to use metaphors and vivid imagery to convey complex emotions and ideas. His works are also characterized by their focus on the beauty of nature and the divine.

‘Meghadootam’ takes the form of a poem in which a cloud, banished from its homeland, sends a message to his beloved. The poem is a meditation on the power of love and the pain of separation, and is widely regarded as one of the most moving works of Indian literature.

‘Meghadootam’ is a beautiful and poetic creation that provides an insight into the life of a Yaksha who is exiled from his beloved. It is about a Yaksha who has been separated from his wife and is living a life of loneliness and despair in a mountain. One day, he comes across a cloud and requests it to take a message to his wife. The rest of the poem is about the journey of the cloud and the message it delivers.

One of the most significant lines of the poem is "Sakshatvatapi sannibhutabhuvo nabhah" which means the sky appears to be as if it has come down to earth. This line highlights the importance of nature in our lives. The sky is a symbol of vastness and infinity, and it creates a feeling of awe and wonder in our hearts. When the sky appears to descend to the earth, it gives us a sense of closeness to nature. It makes us realize that nature is not distant from us but is a part of us, and we are a part of it.

Another notable line in the poem is "Antahpuragatam riktapravasah" which refers to the Yaksha's journey from his palace to the mountain, which is depicted as a difficult and challenging one. The line signifies the hardships of life and the pain of separation. The Yaksha's exile from his beloved is not just physical but emotional too. It is a journey of self-discovery, and he learns to appreciate the beauty of life.

The line "Tauyasam mrigarajonakulataa rochayanti" means that the sight of the clouds is so heavenly that it pleases even the animals. This line emphasizes the beauty of nature, and how it has the power to bring happiness to all beings. Even the animals, who have no means to express their emotions, can feel the beauty of nature, and it brings joy to their hearts.

Meghadootam is a masterpiece of poetry that highlights the beauty of nature, the hardships of life, and the universal emotions of love and separation. It teaches us to appreciate the little things in life, to find beauty in simplicity, and to cherish our relationships. The lines of this poem are timeless, and they hold a universal message for all generations. It reminds us that even in our darkest moments, nature has the power to heal our souls and bring us back to life.

Kalidasa's work has influenced generations of writers and poets, both in India and across the world. His unique style, which combines simplicity with depth, has made him a beloved figure in the world of literature. He is also known as Indian Shakespeare.

His works are timeless masterpieces that continue to capture the imagination of readers of all time. No matter how much time passes, it can be said without doubt that the poetic universe created by Kalidasa will continue to stimulate the world for ever.

"Poets are the priests of the Invisible"

II

Jayadeva - The Creator of Eternal Gita Govinda

"There is no greater warrior than
A mother protecting her child."

Jayadeva Kavi also known as Jayadeva Goswami, a Sanskrit poet who was one amongst the "Pancharatna Kavis" (five pirl poets), in the court of King Laxman Sena, the ruler of Vanga Desa(parts of present Bengal and Odisha) during 12th century. Later, he moved to Puri, where he composed his famous work *'Gita Govinda'* at the Jagannath Temple.

"Chandana charchita neela kalebara,
peeta vasana vanamala
Shyama kunda ambu rasi chayaya,
tadit ruchi suchimani"

The above most famous verses of the Gita Govinda describes the beauty of Krishna, who is said to be adorned with sandalwood paste and wearing blue garments with a garland of forest flowers around his neck. He is standing by a dark pool of water, which reflects his image like a shining jewel. The verse captures the essence of the Gita Govinda, which celebrates the divine love between Krishna and Radha in vivid and sensuous imagery. Jayadeva's poetry continues to inspire readers and musicians, and the Gita Govinda remains one of the most beloved works of Indian literature.

Jayadeva, is widely known for his magnum opus the "Gita Govinda," an epic poem that portrays the divine love of Radha and Krishna. Jayadeva was a multifaceted personality who made significant contributions to medieval Indian literature in languages such as Sanskrit and Odia.

Born in the 12th century in a Brahmin family in Kenduli Sasan in Odisha, Jayadeva was well-versed in Vedic scriptures, music, and dance. There is also an argument that Jayadeva was born in a

Buddhist family.

Jayadeva's teachings have also had a significant impact on Indian spirituality and philosophy. His works emphasize the importance of devotion and surrender to God, and his poetry celebrates the beauty and divinity of nature. Jayadeva's teachings have been embraced by many spiritual leaders and have inspired countless people to seek a deeper connection with the divine.

The Gita Govinda consists of twelve cantos, each containing twenty-four verses written in Sanskrit language, and describes the eternal love between Lord Krishna and Radha. The poem is characterized by vivid imagery, lyrical beauty, and musicality, and it gained immense popularity amongst devotees of Lord Krishna.

In Gita Govinda, Jayadeva portrays Radha-Krishna's love in various situations, such as the initial attraction, the longing, the union, and the separation. He beautifully describes the emotions, sentiments, and feelings of the lovers and the dolorous agony of their separation. The Gita Govinda presented the erotic aspect of Bhakti to the readers and glorifies the physical relationship of lovers as a sacred union between the Jivatma and the Paramatma.

Jayadeva's contribution to Indian literature was not limited to Gita Govinda. He also wrote a commentary on the Brahma Sutras, as well as other works like Chandraloka, Keshavamrita, and Dashavatara Charitam. He was known for his ability to write in multiple languages, including Manipravalam, Sanskrit, and Odia.

Jayadeva's literary work did not only have a significant impact on Indian classical literature but also on Indian classical dance and music. The Gita Govinda's verses served as inspiration to many dance forms, including Odissi and Bharatanatyam. His poems were set to music as well, and many composers rendered them in classical Indian music forms.

Jayadeva was a celebrated poet, dancer, and musician who made significant contributions to Indian classical literature. His Gita Govinda is still an inspiration for many people today and continues to impress generations with its lyrical beauty and poetic excellence. Jayadeva's legacy lives on in the world of literature, dance, and music, where his creations will continue to inspire generations of readers, dancers and musicians for centuries to come.

Poetry ... is the revelation of a feeling that the poet believes to be interior and personal which the reader recognizes as his own."

III

Kabir Das - A Mystic Poet of India

"Kasturi Kundal Base, Mrug Dhoondhe Ban Maahi,
Aise Ghati Ghati Ram Hain, Duniya Janat Nahin Naahi."

The above lines born from the pen of famous philosophical poet Kabir Das epitomize his philosophy.

Through this couplet, Kabir Das wants to convey that just as musk (which is a fragrant substance) permeates the navel of a deer and attracts it to run around the forest in search of the source of the fragrance, similarly, humans also keep searching for God in various places, but fail to understand that God is omnipresent in every particle of the universe. This concept is difficult for common man to comprehend.

Kabir Das beautifully illustrates the human quest for God through the metaphor of the deer's search for musk. He highlights the fact that just as the deer is drawn to the fragrance of musk, humans are drawn to the idea of God and keep searching for Him in various places. However, the truth is that God is omnipresent and exists in every particle of the universe. This profound concept is beyond human comprehension.

Kabir, the medieval Indian poet-saint, was born in the fifteenth century in Varanasi, Uttar Pradesh. Though there are many legends around his taking birth, his verses cast a vivid light on the life and times he lived in. He was a weaver by profession, and his poems were composed in the everyday language spoken by the common people. The power of his poetry lies in his ability to express profound spiritual truths in the simplest of terms. As a result, his verses resonate across generations, cultures, and languages, touching people's hearts and minds. Kabir's poetry is characterized by its simplicity and directness. He wrote in a vernacular form of Hindi that was accessible to the common people, and his verses were often sung by wandering minstrels. Kabir's poetry is steeped in mysticism, and his work often explores the nature of God, the universe, and the human condition.

Kabir's poems are an amalgamation of Bhakti and Sufi philosophy, and he propagated the idea of inner spirituality. His verses were not limited to one particular religion or belief system, but as a weaver, he used everyday similes and metaphors to bring out the essence of his verse. His poems touched upon several themes, including love, devotion, the futility of rituals, the trap of Maya, the importance of the master, and the path to enlightenment.

Kabir wrote "Dohas' too. Doha means the lyrical verse-format which was extensively used by Indian poets and bards of North India probably since the beginning of the 6th century AD. Kabir composed Dohas simple yet profound thoughts on the human condition.

For example, one of his couplets reads,

"Dukh Mein Sumiran Sab Kare, Sukh Mein Kare Na Koye.
Sukh Mein Sumiran Jo Kare, Dukh Kaahe Ko Hoye?"

It means that it is easier for us to remember the divine in times of sorrow but difficult in times of happiness. However, if we remember the divine in times of joy, then there will be no sorrow.

Similarly his another Doha;

"Moko Kahan Dhunde Re Bande, Main To Tere Paas Mein,
Na Teerath Mein, Na Moorat Mein, Na Ekant Niwas Mein."

It is a beautiful expression of devotion and faith in the divine. It speaks of the search for the divine, not in external places such as pilgrimage sites or idols, but within oneself. It is simple yet profound, and it conveys a message that is relevant even today. It reminds us that the true essence of spirituality lies not in external rituals or practices, but in the purity of our hearts and the sincerity of our devotion.

Kabir's poetry was not limited to spiritual and philosophical themes. He was also a social reformer who raised his voice against the caste system, superstitions, and religious dogmas of his time. His poetry was a powerful tool to challenge the status quo and promote social equality and universal brotherhood. His famous lines 'Chinta aisee dakini, kat kalejaye aath, kaal kare so aaj kar, aaj kare so ab' (Worry is such a monster that it eats away eight days a week. What you have to do tomorrow, do it today. What you have to do today, do it now) emphasize the value of time and productivity.

Kabir's poetry is characterized by a number of recurring themes. One of the most prominent is his belief in the unity of all things. Kabir saw God as present in all aspects of creation, and he believed that all beings are ultimately one.

This idea is expressed in one of his most famous poems, which begins:

"Jab Main tha tab hari nahin, ab hari hain main nahin"

It means 'when I was, Hari was not; Now Hari is, I am not'.

Another recurring theme in Kabir's poetry is the importance of spiritual practice. Kabir believed that it was not enough to simply believe in God; one must also cultivate a personal relationship with the divine through prayer, meditation, and self-discipline. He also emphasized the importance of living a virtuous life, and his poems often extolled the virtues of humility, compassion, and service to others.

Kabir was a true mystic poet, whose work transcends religious boundaries and speaks to the universal human experience. His poems are a testament to the power of the human spirit, and his message of love and unity is as relevant today as it was in his time.

Through his poetry, Kabir has left a lasting legacy that continues to inspire and uplift people around the world. Kabir's contribution to literature and society is truly immeasurable. His works have inspired countless generations of poets, mystics, and social reformers. Kabir was a trailblazer who challenged the religious and social conventions of his time, paving the way for a more progressive and inclusive society. His legacy continues to inspire and influence people from all walks of life, and his impact on literature and society is undeniable. We must continue to honor and complete Kabir's vision by promoting his works and spreading his message of love, unity, and equality.

Kabir's poems exemplify the universal nature of spiritual experiences that are pertinent to individuals from all walks of life, regardless of their location or time period. The depth of his work lies in his remarkable ability to capture the essence of these experiences and convey them through his poetry. Kabir's words resonate with readers on a profound level, inspiring them to reflect on their own spiritual journeys and connect with the divine in a more meaningful way. His poetry serves as a timeless reminder of the power of spirituality and its ability to transcend cultural and societal boundaries.

The butterfly counts not months but moments, and has time enough."

IV

Mira Bai - The Saint Poetess from Rajasthan

"Mere To Giridhar Gopal,
Dusra Na Koi.
Jo Sharan Lagat Man Mero,
Tyagat Janam Janam Ka Dukh Hoy"

What to call the state where the devotee evolves to equal status with God? If there is such a word, its synonym is Mira Bai, the saint poetess of India from the land of desert Rajasthan. The quoted line above are from one of Mira Bai's most famous poem "Mere to Giridhar Gopal".

It means:

My only faithful protector is Giridhar Gopal, There is no one else.

Whoever takes refuge in my heart, Leaves behind suffering that lasts for countless lifetimes

Mira Bai, the 16th-century saint-poetess, is known for her soulful devotional poetry in the Bhakti tradition. Her songs express her deep devotion and longing for Krishna, who she sees as her beloved, and her yearning for union with him.

Mira Bai was a member of the Mewar dynasty of Rajasthan. Her husband was Bhoja Raja, the king of Mewar. Bhojaraja and other relatives of Mirabai died in the war with the Mughals. The story goes that the king who came later tried to eliminate Mira bai in various ways but he could not succeeded in that.

Mira Bai expresses her complete surrender to Krishna and sings of his infinite grace and protection. The words "mere to" indicate her personal relationship with Krishna, which is all-absorbing and exclusive. The phrase "giridhar Gopal" refers to Krishna as the lifter of the mountain, which is a reference to the legend of Krishna lifting the Govardhan Hill to save his devotees from a devastating storm. Mira Bai sees Krishna as the one who rescues her from the storms of life and gives her strength and solace.

The second line of the poem, "There is no one else" emphasizes

Mira Bai's conviction that there is no one else worth turning to for protection or support. Her devotion to Krishna is single-minded and unwavering. She sees him as the ultimate source of all goodness and joy and is absorbed in his love. She leads her entire life by meditating on Krishna and praising him with bhajans, and thinking that there is no bode else except him.

The third and fourth lines of the poem express Mira Bai's conviction that turning to Krishna brings an end to all suffering. She believes that taking refuge in his heart is the only way to escape the cycle of birth and death and find true happiness. For Mira Bai, the path of devotion is not just a means of seeking personal liberation but a way to serve and please Krishna, the beloved of her soul.

Overall, Mira Bai's poem "Mere to Giridhar Gopal" is a beautiful expression of her single-minded devotion to Krishna and her trust in his infinite grace and protection. Through her words, she invites us to recognize the divinity within and turn to the divine with unwavering faith and love. Her poetry continues to inspire and uplift us, reminding us of the power of devotion and the beauty of a life dedicated to the divine.

Mira Bai's poetry is characterized by its simplicity and directness, and its focus on the love of Lord Krishna. Her poetry was composed in Rajasthani and Braj Bhasha, the language of the Krishna bhakti tradition. Her songs and poems are still sung and recited today, and they continue to inspire devotees of Lord Krishna across India and beyond.

Mira Bai also wrote that; "Payoji Maine Ram Ratan Dhan Payo" - This devotional line is a tribute to Lord Rama and his qualities of compassion and grace. "Aisi Lagi Lagan" - In this poem, Mira Bai describes her deep yearning for Lord Krishna and the intensity of her love for him.

Mira Bai's impact on Indian literature and culture cannot be overstated. Her poetry represents a profound expression of devotion and faith, and it has inspired countless devotees of Lord Krishna over the centuries. Mira Bai's message of love and devotion to the divine continues to resonate with people across India and around the world, and her poetry remains an enduring testament to the power of faith and devotion.

Mira Bai's teachings emphasize the importance of devotion to God and the need to surrender oneself completely to him. She believed that the love of God was the highest goal of human existence, and that one should strive to achieve this goal through prayer, meditation, and devotion. Mira Bai's poetry is an expression of this devotion, and it continues to serve as a source of inspiration and guidance for those who seek to deepen their relationship with God.

In addition to her poetry, Mira Bai is also known for her life of devotion and service. She is said to have spent much of her life traveling and spreading the message of Krishna bhakti, and she is remembered as a saint and a spiritual leader. Mira Bai's legacy lives on in the hearts of devotees of Lord Krishna, and her poetry continues to inspire and uplift people around the world.

Mira Bai's poetry continued to inspire generations of poets and lovers of bhakti poetry. Her unique style and devotion to Lord Krishna have made her one of the most celebrated poets of India. Her life and work have been the subject of numerous books, films, and plays, and her bhajans are still sung in temples and homes across the country.

Her poetry has been translated into several languages and has been an inspiration to poets and musicians across the world. Mira Bai's legacy continues to live on, as her work continues to inspire people to this day. Her life was immersed in devotion to Krishna and by composing and singing bhajans, Mirabai made her life equal to a devotional song.

ꟈ

I have given up the world to follow your footsteps;
My Master, I have become your disciple."

ꟈ

V

Mir Taqi Mir - The Poet of Urdu Gazals

Mir Taqi Mir, a poet of 18th Century was one of the most celebrated poets of the Urdu language. He lived during a time of great political and social upheaval in India, as the Mughal Empire was in decline and various regional powers vied for control. Despite this, Mir's poetry was not overtly political, instead focusing on themes of love, mysticism, and the beauty of the natural world. His work is considered some of the finest in the Urdu language, and his influence can be seen in the works of countless poets who followed in his footsteps.

Mir was born into a family of poets and scholars, and he began composing poetry at a young age. He was highly educated, studying both Arabic and Persian literature, as well as the works of Indian poets. Despite his privileged background, Mir's life was marked by tragedy and hardship. He lost his father at a young age, and he experienced the death of several of his children. He also struggled with poverty throughout much of his life, as his poetry did not bring him the financial success he had hoped for.

Despite these difficulties, Mir's poetry continued to resonate with readers. His most famous works are his ghazals, a form of poetry usually set to music, that originated in Persia and became popular in India during the Mughal period. Ghazals are short poems consisting of rhyming couplets that explore themes of love and spirituality.

Mir's ghazals are characterized by their exquisite language, vivid imagery, and profound emotional depth. They explore the nature of love in all its forms, from the ecstatic joy of new love to the agony of separation and loss.

Mir's poetry also explores themes of mysticism. He was a devout Muslim, and his poetry often reflects his deep faith. Many of his poems are addressed to God, whom he describes in intimate and personal terms. He also draws on the imagery and symbolism of Sufism, a mystical branch of Islam that emphasizes the pursuit of spiritual knowledge and the attainment of union with the divine.

Mir's impact on Urdu literature cannot be overstated. He is considered one of the greatest poets in the language, and his influence can be seen in the works of countless writers who followed in his footsteps. His poetry has been translated into many languages, including English, and continues to be read and celebrated today. His legacy has also been honoured in various ways, such as the establishment of the Mir Taqi Mir Award for Urdu literature.

rāh-e-dūr-e-ishq meñ rotā hai kyā
aage aage dekhiye hotā hai kyā
"Does one weep on the path to the distant beloved?
Come, look ahead and see what will happen."

The couplet written by Mir reflects on the pain and difficulty one may face on the path of love. The phrase "rāh-e-dūr-e-ishq" refers to the path of love, which is often long and arduous. The poet questions whether one cries or weeps on this path, suggesting that the journey may be filled with sorrow and tears. However, he also encourages the reader to look ahead and see what lies ahead on this path, implying that the journey may ultimately lead to happiness and fulfilment. Overall, the couplet conveys a sense of hope and perseverance in the face of the challenges that may arise on the path of love.

Some of his other famous couplets:

ishq ik 'mīr' bhārī patthar hai
kab ye tujh nā-tavāñ se uThtā hai
hogā kisī dīvār ke saa.e meñ paḌā 'mīr'
kyā rabt mohabbat se us ārām-talab ko
'mīr' ham mil ke bahut ḳhush hue tum se pyāre
is ḳharābe meñ mirī jaan tum ābād raho

In addition to his literary contributions, Mir's life and work also provide insight into the social and cultural context of his time. His poetry reflects the complex and diverse society of India during the Mughal period, with its blend of Indian, Persian, and Islamic influences. It also sheds light on the experiences of the elite classes, as well as the struggles of the common people. Mir's poetry, therefore, not only offers a glimpse into the individual human experience but also into the broader historical and cultural context in which he lived.

Mir Taqi Mir was a poet whose work continues to resonate with readers today. His exquisite language, profound emotional depth, and exploration of universal themes such as love and spirituality have earned him a place as one of Mir Taqi Mir's poetry had a profound impact on the Urdu literary scene and has continued to inspire generations of poets.

He is widely considered one of the greatest poets in the Urdu language and his works continue to be celebrated for their beauty, depth, and insight. His influence can be seen in the works of many contemporary poets, including Gulzar, Javed Akhtar, and Nida Fazli.

Mir Taqi Mir's contribution to Urdu poetry cannot be overstated. He brought a new level of refinement and sophistication to the ghazal, elevating it to a form of high art. His poetry is characterized by its lyricism, emotional depth, and philosophical insight. He explored themes such as love, faith, spirituality, and the human condition, offering a unique perspective on these timeless subjects.

One of Mir's most famous ghazals is "Dil-e-Nadan Tujhe Hua Kya Hai," which translates to *"Oh foolish heart, what has happened to you?"* In this ghazal, Mir addresses his own heart, which he personifies as a separate entity from himself. He laments the pain that his heart has experienced in love, and he wonders why it continues to seek out love even though it knows the pain it will bring. Like many of Mir's works, this also speaks to the universal human experience of love and loss.

Mir's poems, explores the theme of love and the pain that often accompanies it. His words "dil-e-nadan" (innocent heart) suggest that the speaker is addressing someone who is naive or inexperienced in matters of the heart. The second line asks a rhetorical question, implying that there is no cure for the pain of love.

Mir's poetry is marked by its musicality and rhythm. His use of meter and rhyme is masterful, and his words often seem to dance off the page. His works are full of alliteration, assonance, and other poetic devices that add to the beauty and musicality of his verse.

In addition to his contributions to Urdu poetry, Mir Taqi Mir was also an important figure in the cultural and intellectual life of eighteenth-century India. He was a member of the Delhi literary circle, which included other notable writers such as Mirza Ghalib, and was known for his erudition and wit. His poetry was widely appreciated by the ruling elites, and he was a favorite of the Mughal Emperor Muhammad Shah.

Despite his success and influence, Mir's life was not without its share of difficulties. He struggled with poverty and ill health for much of his life, and suffered personal tragedies, like death of his young son. These bitter experiences also undoubtedly contributed to the depth and emotional power of his poetry.

Mir Taqi Mir's legacy continues to live on today, and his works remain an important part of the Urdu literary canon. His poetry has been translated into many languages, including English, and continues to inspire and captivate readers around the world.

In recognition of his contributions to literature, the Government of India has named several institutions and awards after him, including the Mir Taqi Mir Award for Urdu Poetry.

ജ

"To be a poet is a condition, not a profession."

ജ

VI

Mirza Ghalib - The Legend of Urdu Poetry

Mirza Ghalib is one of the most prominent poets of the Indian subcontinent. He was born on December 27, 1797, in Agra, India, and his real name was Mirza Asadullah Baig Khan. Ghalib is known for his exquisite poetry and his unique style that is characterized by his use of Urdu and Persian languages, as well as his philosophical, mystical, and romantic themes. His poetry is widely regarded as some of the greatest and most beautiful in the Urdu language, and his impact on the literary world cannot be overstated.

Ghalib grew up in Delhi and was educated in Persian and Arabic, which were the dominant languages of the Mughal court. He began writing poetry at a young age and was quickly recognized for his talent. Ghalib's poetry is deeply influenced by the events of his life, including the fall of the Mughal Empire, his personal struggles, and his love affairs. He was a master of the ghazal, a form of poetry that consists of rhyming couplets and is often used to express themes of love and beauty.

One of Ghalib's most famous works is his collection of poems called the Diwan-e-Ghalib. This collection includes his most famous ghazals, "Ishq mujhko nahi wehshat hi sahi," "Hazaaron khwahishein aisi," "Aah ko chahiye ek umr asar hone tak" etc. In these poems, Ghalib explores themes of love, loss, longing, and the transience of life. His poetry is deeply introspective and often uses complex imagery and metaphors to express his ideas.

The poem 'I will not Cry' begins with the following lines;

"I will not cry for satisfaction if I could get my choice,
Among the divine beautiful virgins of heaven, I want only you.
After killing me, do not bury me in your street,
Why should people know your home address with my reference."

In another poem he wrote;

"Heart it is, not a brick or stone
Why shouldn't it feel the pain?
Let none tyrannize this heart
Or I shall cry again and again?"

Ghalib's style of poetry is characterized by its simplicity, elegance, and beauty. His language is rich and expressive, and his verses are often filled with complex imagery and metaphors. His poetry is often deeply personal, reflecting his own experiences and emotions, but it is also universal in its appeal, addressing themes that are common to all human beings.

Ghalib's impact on Urdu literature and culture cannot be overstated. He is regarded as one of the greatest poets in the history of the Urdu language, and his influence on the development of Urdu poetry has been profound. His poetry has inspired generations of poets and continues to be widely read and appreciated today.

In addition to his contributions to literature, Ghalib was also an important figure in the cultural and political life of his time. He was a close friend of the last Mughal emperor, Bahadur Shah Zafar, and was deeply involved in the events leading up to the Indian Rebellion of 1857. His poetry often reflects his political views, and he was a vocal critic of the British colonial government and its policies in India.

Ghalib's legacy continues to be felt today, both in India and Pakistan, where Urdu is an official language. His poetry has been translated into many languages and is read and appreciated around the world. He remains an important figure in the cultural and literary history of the Indian subcontinent, and his influence on Urdu literature and culture is still evident today.

In addition to his literary and cultural contributions, Ghalib was also a teacher and mentor to many aspiring poets. His teachings on the art of poetry and his philosophy of life continue to be studied and admired by scholars and enthusiasts alike. Ghalib's approach to poetry was deeply rooted in his own experiences, and he often emphasized the importance of sincerity, passion, and personal expression in the art of poetry.

Ghalib's style of poetry was characterized by the use of simple language and the clever use of metaphor, which gave his verses a timeless quality. He was a master of the ghazal form, which is a poetic form that consists of rhyming couplets and a refrain. In his ghazals, Ghalib was able to convey complex emotions and ideas with great ease and elegance. His verses were often melancholic, reflecting the pain and suffering that he experienced in his personal life. He was also a master of the qasida form, which is a long poem that is often used to praise a patron or ruler.

Ghalib's impact on Urdu poetry and literature cannot be overstated. He is considered to be one of the greatest poets in the history of the Urdu language and his work continues to be studied and admired by scholars and enthusiasts alike. His poetry has inspired generations of writers and poets, and his influence can be seen in the works of many modern Urdu poets. Ghalib's poetry has also been translated into many languages, including English, and has been widely read and appreciated by readers around the world.

In addition to his contributions to Urdu poetry, Ghalib was also a prominent figure in the cultural and social life of his time. He was known for his humorr sense and intelligence, and his poetry often commented on the political and social issues of his days. He was a close friend of many prominent figures of the time, including the last Mughal emperor, Bahadur Shah Zafar, and he was also a regular attendee of the mushairas, or poetry gatherings, that were popular in that period.

Ghalib's poetry often reflected his belief in the power of language to transcend the limitations of the self and connect people to one another. He believed that poetry had the power to reveal the hidden truths of the universe and to help people find meaning and purpose in their lives. His poetry was often infused with a sense of spirituality, and he frequently explored the themes of love, faith, and the human condition in his work.

His work continues to be studied and admired by scholars and enthusiasts alike, and his influence can be seen in the works of many modern Urdu poets. His impact on Urdu literature and culture is immeasurable, and his legacy continues to inspire and captivate readers around the world.

"Without language, one cannot talk to people and understand them; one cannot share their hopes and aspirations, grasp their history, appreciate their poetry, or savor their songs."

VII

Rabindranath Tagore - The Universal Poet from India

"Before you I have no cause
To be vain about my art
O master poet, at your feet I give up
All pride in my craft!
Let me dedicate my life
And make a flute that is plain
Let me fill its stops
With tunes all my own"

These are the famous lines from Gitanjali written by Rabindranath Tagore who was known as the universal poet of India. Rabindranath Tagore is a name that resounds with the essence of Indian literature. He is one of the most celebrated writers in the world and his works are an inspiration to generations for all time. His unique perspective on life and his dedication to literature are notable in the poetic history of India.

Rabindranath Tagore was born in Calcutta, India, in 1861. Tagore was home-schooled and his early education was in Bengali, Sanskrit, and English. He later attended University College, London, but dropped out after a year. He returned to India and started writing.

In 1913, Tagore became the first non-European to receive the Nobel Prize in Literature, for his collection of poems 'Gitanjali'. The collection was translated into English by himself, and it was a significant milestone in the literary history of India.

Tagore's literary contributions are numerous, including about 100 collections of 3,000 poems, 2,300 songs, 50 plays, art books, and collections of essays. His poetic journey began with the publication of his first book of poems, called Sandhya Sangit, in 1882. His poetry is a beautiful reflection of the human condition, and his mastery of the language is evident in the way he weaves words together. Apart from the above, he drew more than 3000 pictures.

'Janganamana' and 'Amar Shonar Bangla', both born from the pen of Tagore later became the national anthems of India and Bangladesh respectively. He was one of those rare geniuses who influenced the history of the Indian freedom struggle from behind the scenes.

One of his most beautiful poems is "The Gardener", a collection of love poems that explore the emotional depths of love and longing. The Gardener reflects the beauty of nature, the solitude of the human heart, and the complexities of human relationships. Many of his other works, such as Gitanjali, Song Offerings, and The Crescent Moon, reflect his spiritual journey and his search for truth.

Tagore's dedication to his work was evident in his establishment of Santiniketan, a small town in West Bengal, India, where he founded a school called Abode of Peace. Santiniketan became a center for intellectuals, artists, and scholars who shared Tagore's vision. He believed in the idea of education as a means of social reform and cultural rejuvenation.

Rabindranath Tagore, the great Indian philosopher and writer, is renowned for his exceptional contributions to literature. His poetry, in particular, stands out for its insightful messages about life, nature, and human relationships. His poems are known for their simplicity and their power to touch the hearts of readers. This essay will explain some of his poems and provide a few lines from each to illustrate how they capture the essence of his themes.

One of Tagore's most famous poems, "*Where the Mind is Without Fear,*" reflects his vision of a free and united India. The poem expresses the poet's deep desire for a country where people are not divided by caste or religion and where everyone is treated as equals. The following are a few lines from the poem that explain this message:

"Where the mind is without fear and the head is held high
Where knowledge is free
Where the world has not been broken up into fragments
By narrow domestic walls."

The poem *"The Child"* captures the essence of innocence and beauty in childhood. It has a childlike simplicity that makes it easy for everyone to understand. In the poem, the poet describes how a child leaves behind all fears and worries and lives life to the fullest. Here are a few lines of this poem:

"When the heart is young, when the soul is pure,
The world is a happy place, bright and sure."

Another famous poem is "*Endless Time,*" which explores the concept of continuity and the eternal nature of life. It speaks about the interconnectedness of everything in existence and reflects on the beauty of the never-ending cycle of life. Here are a few lines to explain the idea behind this poem:

"Time is endless in thy hands, my lord.
There is none to count thy minutes.
Days and nights pass and ages bloom and fade like flowers."

Tagore's poems often reflect on relationships between people, particularly those between men and women. In "Love's Gift," he explains the importance of communication and trusts in love. The poem conveys the message that love, like a gift, needs to be given and received freely, without any expectations. Here are a few lines:

"Love's gift cannot be given it waits to be accepted."

Finally, "The Journey" is a poem that reflects on the human experience of life. The poem speaks of the journey of life as a traveler on the path of time. It speaks of the need to embrace life's experiences and accept them as they come. The poem's lines reflect the message of the poem:

"I have spent my days stringing and unstringing my instrument while the song I came to sing remains unsung."

Rabindranath Tagore's works are a reflection of the beauty and complexities of life. His poetry is a testament to his genius and dedication to literature. His works continue to inspire and influence people across the globe, and his legacy lives on through the literary tradition he established. As he once said, *"I slept and dreamt that life was joy. I awoke and saw that life was service. I acted and behold, service was joy."*. He was a wonderful genius who combined various aspects of culture and was always the priest of optimistic faith, love of the world and nationalism.

"Do not ask which creatures are made of the same material as you. The best ones are those who nourish you."

VIII

Sarojini Naidu - The Nightingale of India

Sarojini Naidu, known as the Nightingale of India, was one of the leading voices of the Indian independence movement, and one of the most prominent poets of her time. Born on February 13, 1879, in Hyderabad, Naidu was a gifted child and excelled in academics. She was educated at King's College London and Girton College, Cambridge, where she studied literature and the arts.

Naidu began writing poetry at a young age and published her first collection of poems, "The Golden Threshold," in 1905. The collection was well-received and established her as a poet of note. Her poetry was marked by a rich lyricism and a musical quality, and she was known for her use of imagery and metaphor. Naidu's poetry was deeply influenced by the romantic poets, and she often wrote about love, nature, and the beauty of the world around her.

Naidu's most famous poems include "The Song of Radha," "In the Forest," and "Indian Weavers." Her poetry has been translated into many languages and is widely read and admired throughout the world. *A Love song from the North, A Rajput Love Song, Alabaster, An Indian Love Song, Autumn song, Corn Grinders, Coromandel Fishers, Cradle Song, Ectasy, Harvest Hymn, Humayun To Zobeida, In Praise of Henna, In Salutation to the Eternal Peace, Indian Dancer, Leili, Life, My Dead Dream, Nightfall in the City of Hyderabad, To Youth, The Snake Charmer, Village Song, Wandering Singers, Street Cries, Suttee, Palanquin Bearers*etc. are other notable Poems of Naidu.

The poem, 'In the Forest' starts with the following lines:

"Here, O my hear, let us burn the dear dreams that are dead,
Here in this wood let us fashion a funeral pyre
Of fallen white petals and leaves that are mellow and red,
Here let us burn them in noon's flaming torches of fire"

In addition to her literary accomplishments, Naidu was also a prominent figure in the Indian freedom movement. She was a close associate of Mahatma Gandhi and played an active role in the nonviolent struggle for Indian independence.

Mahatma Gandhi named her the 'Nightingale of India' because of the beauty of her poems. Sarojini Naidu was the first woman president of the Indian National Congress and the first lady governor of India.

Naidu's poetry was not limited to themes of love and beauty, however. She was also a political activist and a leader in the Indian independence movement. She was an ardent supporter of Mahatma Gandhi's nonviolent resistance, and her poetry often reflected her political beliefs. In *"The Indian Weavers,"* she writes about the plight of Indian weavers who were struggling under the British colonial regime:

"Weavers, weaving at brek of day,
Why do you weave a garment so gay? . . .
Weavers, weaving sorrow and pain,
Dyeing the threads of their warp in vain."

Naidu was also an accomplished orator, and her speeches were known for their eloquence and passion. She was the first woman to be elected president of the Indian National Congress, and she played an important role in the negotiations that led to India's independence from British rule.

In addition to her poetry and political activism, Naidu was also a prominent figure in the world of literature. She was a close friend of many of the leading writers and poets of her time, including Rabindranath Tagore and W.B. Yeats. She was also a prolific writer of prose, and her books on Indian culture and folklore are still widely read.

Naidu's poetry and writing helped to shape the cultural identity of India during a period of great change and upheaval, and her contributions to the Indian independence movement were instrumental in securing India's freedom. Her legacy continues to inspire poets, writers, and activists today, and her influence can be seen in the works of many contemporary Indian writers.

Naidu's impact on Indian literature and culture is immeasurable. Her poetry continues to inspire and move people around the world, and her legacy as a freedom fighter and political leader is an important part of Indian history. She remains one of the most beloved and respected figures in Indian literature and culture, and her contributions to both fields will never be forgotten.

Sarojini Naidu was a remarkable poet, political activist, and cultural figure. Her poetry was marked by lyrical beauty and a deep love for India and its people, and her political activism helped to shape the course of Indian history. Her legacy as the Nightingale of India continues to inspire and uplift people today, and her contributions to Indian literature and culture are an enduring part of the country's rich cultural heritage.

ꕥ

"The only way to combat death is to live life to the fullest."

ꕥ

IX

Subramania Bharathi - The Pioneer of Modern Tamil Poetry

"When will this thirst for freedom slake?
When will our love of slavery die?
When will our Mother's fetters break?
When will our tribulations cease?"

A strong desire for freedom and equality which awakens from the deep heart will always raise questions against slavery and inequality. The poetic voice of Mahakavi Subrahmanya Bharathi, which spread through the rural villages of Tamil Nadu raised such strong questions and pleaded for social justice and equality, later turned as an unforgettable voice of the history of freedom struggle in India.

Subramania Bharathi, a freedom fighter, journalist and above all the well known poetical voice from the State of Tamil Nadu, whose poetry shook the forts of British Empire. He also known as Bharathiyar and Mahakavi Bharathi, was a passionate Tamil poet who lived from 1882 to 1921. Within a short span of 39 mortal years, he became the voice of Tamil modern poetry. He was a prolific writer who composed poetry on a wide range of themes, including patriotism, social justice, and spirituality.

In many of his poems Bharathi emphasizes the importance of freedom and equality and social justice amongst the society, regardless of their caste, race, occupation, or social status. He highlights the injustices faced by outcastes, fishermen, nomads, and tribes and calls for their freedom.

Bharathi also advocates for a society where people get good education and can engage in skilled work without harming others. He envisions a world where the society leads a peaceful life without any discrimination or oppression.

For him, poetry is none other than a platform to rouse the sleeping masses of our Country. His poetry and writings played a significant role in India's freedom struggle and continue to inspire the nation even today.

Subramania Bharathi's poem "Vande Mataram," expresses his patriotism which he wrote in 1908 as a tribute to the motherland. Some of its verses goes like this:

"Here flourish a thousand castes,
But no room for foreigners
The Mother's children may quarrel,
Yet they are brothers.
What is life without unity?
Division only spells ruin.
If we hold fast to this truth,
What more can we need?"

The above lines express who is Subrahmanya Bharathi and for what object he raises his poetic voice. The puranic lore of India inspired him always and he believes that his work itself is poetry, eternal vigilance and service to the nation.

Subramania Bharathi being an Indian writer, poet, journalist, social reformer, and polyglot has played a vital part in the Indian independence movement. Bharathi received his early education in Tirunelveli and Varanasi and later worked as a journalist for several newspapers, including The Hindu, Bala Bharata, Vijaya, Chakravarthini, the Swadesamitran, and India. He is regarded as one of the greatest Tamil literary figures of all time and a pioneer of modern Tamil poetry.

Bharathi was a prolific writer who covered a wide range of themes, including politics, society, and spirituality. His literary influence on

Tamil literature is unparalleled, with his works being widely used in Tamil cinema and becoming staples in the literary and musical repertoire of Tamil artistes worldwide. Despite being proficient in around 32 languages, including three non-Indian foreign languages, Bharathi's favourite language was always Tamil, which he believed was beautiful in nature.

Apart from his literary contributions, Bharathi was a social reformer who fought for women's emancipation, opposed child marriage and the caste system, and advocated for the reform of society and religion. Bharathi's excellence in poetry and his relentless efforts to promote social justice have made him an icon in Tamil Nadu's cultural and political history.

At the age of 11, he was given the title of "Bharathi" by the Raja of Ettayapuram, in recognition of his exceptional talent in poetry.

While he was in Varanasi, Bharathi's exposure to Hindu spirituality and nationalism broadened his perspective, and he learned Sanskrit, Hindi, and English. He also altered his appearance, growing a beard and wearing a turban in admiration of Sikhs, influenced by his Sikh friend.

Bharathi's involvement in the Indian independence movement continued to grow, and he became a vocal advocate for Indian freedom from British colonial rule. He used his poetry and writings to inspire and motivate the people of India to fight for their rights and freedom. He highlighted the importance of self-respect, education, and empowerment of the masses through his poems. He called for a complete boycott of British goods and advocated for the use of Swadeshi products.

Bharathi was also a strong advocate for women's rights and was one of the earliest champions of gender equality in India. He believed that women should be given equal opportunities and that they had a crucial role to play in the development of the country. He encouraged women to become educated and to participate in social and political activities.

Bharathi's contribution to Tamil literature and the Indian freedom struggle remains invaluable. He passed away at the young age of 39 in 1921, but his legacy continues to inspire generations of Indians even today.

During his time in Pondicherry, Bharathi continued to write and publish his works, despite facing censorship and suppression from the British authorities. He also continued to be involved in the Indian independence movement, supporting the revolutionary wing and working closely with leaders such as Aurobindo, Lajpat Rai, and V.V.S. Aiyar.

Bharathi's literary output expanded to include translations of Vedic literature. Some of his well known works are 'Nilavum Vanminum Katrum', 'Kuyil Pattu', 'Panchali Sapatham', and Kannan Pattu.

Bharathi's contributions to Tamil literature and culture have been widely recognized and celebrated. Bharathi's songs are also popular among musicians and have been set to various tunes and styles. Many of his works have been translated into different languages, including English, Hindi, Telugu, Kannada, and Malayalam. His message of nationalism, social reform, and universal brotherhood is inimitable for the present generation.

The establishment of the National Subramanya Bharati Award, Bharathiar University, as well as the various statues, movies, and road names dedicated to him, are testaments to his enduring legacy. There is no doubt that Bharati marks a decisive turning point in the development of Indian poetic tradition.

"There is no greater warrior than a mother protecting her child."

X

Mahadevi Verma - The Queen of Indian Poetry

Mahadevi Verma was one of the most important poets of the era of Neo Romantism movement in modern Hindi literature. She was born in Farrukhabad, Uttar Pradesh. Her poems had a wide acceptance in Hindi literature. She was not only an outstanding poet but also she was deeply involved in the Indian Freedom struggle. Considering her dedicated life to reviving the literature she was termed as 'Queen of Hindi poetry'. She was also referred as Modern Meera. Mahadevi could raise an unparalleled own voice in the Hindi literature.

Mahadevi Verma was born to a wealthy family that valued education, and she received a formal education from a young age. She began writing poetry in her teens and was soon recognized for her talent. In 1927, she published her first collection of poems, titled "Saundarya Lahari" (Intoxicating Beauty). The collection was well received and established her as a rising star in Hindi poetry.

Over the years, Mahadevi Verma's style evolved, becoming more introspective and philosophical. Her later works, such as "Yama" (The God of Death) and "Neeraja" (Lotus), explore themes of mortality, spirituality, and the human condition. She was a prolific writer, penning more than twenty collections of poetry, several plays, and numerous essays and short stories.

Mahadevi Verma's poetry is characterized by its depth, lyricism, and use of nature imagery. Her writing often features the natural world as a metaphor for human experience, as seen in her poem "Madhur Madhur Mere Deepak Jal" (My Lamps Burn Bright and Sweet). Her works are infused with a sense of hope and optimism, despite their often-weighty themes.

High human values, women rights and love towards the fellow creatures etc are applaudable themes reflects in her poems. *"Titali Se" i.e 'To the Butterfly'* is an example of her love towards fellow creatures.

"Meh barasne vaala hai,
Meri Khirkee me aa jaa title
Bahar jab par honge geele
Ghul jaayenge rang sajeele
Jhar jaayega phool na tujko
Bacha sakegaa choti titalee"

It means that 'The rain is about to fall, come through my window, butterfly; Outside when they become wet, your charming colours will melt away; the flower will fall to the ground; it won't be able to save you, small butterfly; come through my window'. The overflowing love towards the fellow creatures can be seen in these lines. In another poem *'Tum mujhme Priya, phir Parichay kya'* means 'Why an introduction, since you are in me' she wrote;

"You are drawn, I am just an outline,
you are the sweet melody, I am just a string of notes,
you are limitless, I am but an illusion of limits,
In the secrecy of real image-reflection,
why enact to be lovers!"

Dedicated love was another important theme reflects in her poems. She had her own unique style of writing which makes her popular in Hindi literature world. She also fought for women rights.

Neehar, Reshmi, Nirja, Sandhya Geet, Deepkshika, Agnirekha, Pratham Aayam, Saptparna, Vividh Kavitayen, Yama, Nilambara, Aatmika, Sandhini etc are her important works. India Government honoured Mahadevi by awarding the prestigious Gyanpeeth Award for the Poetry 'Yama'. Her poetry, social upliftment work, and welfare development among women were all deeply reflected in her writings, which influenced not only readers but also critics, especially her novel Deepshikha.

Mahadevi Verma was also a social activist and feminist, and her poetry reflected her commitment to gender equality and women's empowerment. Her most famous work, "Rashmi Rathi" (Sun's Chariot), is a retelling of the Mahabharata from the perspective of Draupadi, the female protagonist. The poem is a powerful statement on the importance of women's agency and autonomy, and it has become a seminal work in Indian feminist literature.

In addition to her poetry, Mahadevi Verma was also a committed educator. She founded a school for girls in Allahabad in 1937, and she continued to champion women's education throughout her life. She believed that education was the key to social change, and her efforts helped pave the way for generations of Indian women.

Mahadevi Verma's legacy continues to inspire and influence Indian poets and writers. Her commitment to social justice and gender equality, as well as her lyrical and introspective poetry, have made her a beloved figure in Indian literature.

She remains a role model for women and an important voice in the ongoing struggle for equality and empowerment. Her abilities, strength, and resolve lay accessible to all those willing to embrace them, and her legacy will continue to be an influence in the years to come. Her nickname, the *"Queen of Hindi Poetry,"* was well-deserved, and remains an apt tribute to her literary achievements.

"We want deeper sincerity of motive, a greater courage in speech and earnestness in action."

XI

Harivansh Rai Bachchan - Indian Poet of the Century

Harivansh Rai Bachchan, born on November 27, 1907, in Allahabad, India, was a renowned Hindi poet, writer, and scholar. He is regarded as one of the greatest Hindi poets of the 20th century and was also a prominent literary figure in the Indian Independence movement. Bachchan's literary works were known for their simplicity and elegance, and he often wrote about social issues such as poverty, discrimination, and the plight of the common man.

"Kavita se roti nahi paoge,
Par agar Kavita padhoge toh saleeke se khaoge"

("You cannot earn bread from poetry, but if you read poetry,
you will learn to eat with manners.")

This is the principle of Bachchan. It suggests that poetry may not provide a means of material sustenance or monetary gain, but it can enrich a person's life in many other ways. Reading poetry can help to develop one's sensitivity to language and appreciation for aesthetics, which can have a positive impact on personal development and relationships. The phrase also implies that reading poetry can cultivate a sense of refinement and propriety, which can contribute to a more sophisticated and cultured way of living. It also conveys the idea that while creating poetry or creating any other arts may not bring financial stability, however it will enrich the mind and soul of the reader.

Bachchan's famous works include the poetry collections like *Madhushala (The House of Wine), Madhubala (The Honey Bee), and his autobiography, Kya Bhooloon Kya Yaad Karoon (What Shall I Remember, What Shall I Forget?).*

Bachchan's writing style is characterized by a unique blend of traditional Hindi poetry and modernist techniques. His poetry is often described as having a musical quality, with a rhythm and melody that make it both accessible and captivating.

One of Bachchan's most famous works, Madhushala, is a collection of 135 quatrains that celebrate life, love, and the human spirit. The poems in Madhushala are inspired by the taverns of medieval India, where poets and philosophers would gather to drink and discuss their ideas. The collection was an instant hit and is considered a classic of Hindi literature. The poem's central metaphor is the tavern as a symbol of life, with wine representing the joy and sorrows that people experience in their journey. Madhusala is a combination of love, beauty, pain, sorrow, death, life etc. He also wrote songs for many Hindi Films.

Bachchan's other notable works include his translations of William Shakespeare's plays into Hindi, which helped to introduce the works of the Bard to a wider audience in India. He also translated the works of T.S. Eliot, Omar Khayyam, and W.B. Yeats, among others.

Bachchan's impact on Indian literature and culture is immeasurable. His poetry has inspired generations of Hindi writers and readers and has been set to music by many renowned Indian musicians.

Bachchan's use of simple, everyday language in his poetry made it accessible to a wider audience and helped to popularize Hindi literature. His poems are often quoted in popular culture and have become a part of the Indian cultural consciousness.

Bachchan was not only a poet but also a social activist. He actively participated in the Indian Independence movement and used his writing to express his views on social issues like poverty and discrimination. He believed that literature had the power to change society and worked tirelessly to promote the use of Hindi as a national language.

Bachchan's autobiography *'Kya Bhooloon Kya Yaad Karoon'*was translated into English in the name *"In the Afternoon of Time"*. His autobiography went on to become one of the most widely-read autobiographies in Hindi.

Bachchan received numerous honors and awards during his lifetime, including the Padma Bhushan in 1976 and the Sahitya Akademi Award for his autobiography in 1969. He was also nominated for the Nobel Prize in Literature in 1984. Hindi Film Super Star Amitabh Bachchan is the son of Haribans Rai Bachchan.

Bachchan's life and work are a testament to the power of poetry to connect people and to effect change in the world.

☙

"The fragrance of love is always redolent of sacrifice."

☙

XII

Ramdhari Singh Dinkar - The Poet of Courage

Ramdhari Singh Dinkar was a famous poet of Hindi literature, who through his dynamic usage of language and imagery effectively conveyed his message, be it social, political, or spiritual.

He, popularly known as 'Dinkar', was a celebrated Hindi poet, essayist, and academician. He was born in 1908, in Simaria village of Bihar, and breathed his last on 24th April 1974, in New Delhi. His contribution to Hindi and Mythali literature are unparalleled, and he is regarded as one of the greatest Indian poets of the 20th century.

In his poem "Stithi", which was written during the Indian independence struggle he wrote;

Vah Pradeep Jo Dikh Raha Hai Jhilmil, Door Nahi Hai
Thakkar Baith Gaye Kya Bhai! Manzil Door Nahi Hai"

'The lamp that is shining brightly, is not far away;
Have you become tired and sat down, brother?
The destination is not far away."

The poet describes a scene where a light is flickering in the distance, and the destination is not far away from it. Seeing this, the poet says that the goal is not yet achieved, but we have come closer to it. The line *"Thakkar Baith Gaye Kya Bhai!"* means *"Have you become tired and given up, brother?"* The poet emphasizes that we should keep striving towards our goal, not lose hope, and not give up because the destination is not far away.

Dinkar initially was a supporter of revolution but he later turned to Gandhism. He was equally influenced by Mahathma Gandhi and Karal Marx. His famous poem written during Emergency period declared by Smt. Indira Gandhi is well famous. He wrote;

"Simhasan Khaali Karo ge

Janata Aaati Hai"

Vacate the throne, for the people who are coming". This poem was recited by Jaya Prakash Narayan while addressing a huge gathering of people at Ram Lila Maithan of Delhi during Emergency period. Dinakar was a poet of boldness. He had the courage to challenge the thrones and fight for the people which he was done through his poems before and after the Indian Independence.

'Brother of Students' was one of his first poems which was published in a local news paper. Vijay-Sandesh, Birbala and Meghnad-Vadh, Pran-Bhang etc. are his initial poems. 'Renuka' was the first collection of his poems. Rashmirathi and Parashuram ki Prateeksha are also his famous works.

Dinkar was known for his bold and powerful poetry, which had a deep impact on the readers' minds. His works reflected his love for his nation, its culture, values, and history. In his essay 'Sanskriti ke Char Adhyay,' he has described India's rich and ancient culture in four chapters- *Vedas, Upanishads, Ramayana, and Mahabharata*. He believed that India's culture is a continuous process of assimilation, adaptation, and evolution.

Dinkar's poems were not only limited to praising India's glory but also highlighted the social issues and the need for reform. His poem 'Kurukshetra' is an epic description of the Mahabharata's battlefield and the war's aftermath. It is a powerful retelling of the epic, laced with his observations of contemporary society.

Dinkar's most famous poem is 'Urvashi,' which is based on the mythological story of Menaka and Vishwamitra's love affair. The poem depicts the eternal conflict between love and duty and the eternal struggle between material and spiritual wealth.

In essence, Dinkar's poems were an excellent blend of Indian culture, values, and patriotism with contemporary society's social issues. They were not just mere verses but messages that sought to inspire and still a sense of responsibility in the readers' minds.

Dinkar's contributions to Hindi literature did not go unnoticed. He was honored with several awards, including the Padma Bhushan, Sahitya Academy Award, and Jnanpith Award. His poems continue to inspire generations of Hindi readers and are studied as a part of Indian literature.

Ramdhari Singh Dinkar's contributions to Hindi literature were immense. His works were powerful, thought-provoking, and inspiring. Despite being a poet, he was a true patriot who believed in India's rich culture and its potential to build a better society. His poems continue to inspire and influence the readers' minds and will continue to do so for generations to come.

"My grief is like a river of tears, and your memory is the ship that carries me."

XIII

Kumaran Asan - Maha Kavi from Malayalam Language

Kumaran Asan was a prominent Malayalam poet who played a crucial role in the literary and social renaissance of Kerala. Asan initiated a revolution in Malayalam poetryby transforming it from metaphysical to lyrical. He was born on 12th April 1873 in a remote village of Kerala. He considered Sri Narayana Guru, the famous spiritual leader and social reformer of Kerala as his Guru and followed the path of Guru through out his life.

His poetry was characterized by its simplicity, clarity, and lyrical quality. He often wrote about the beauty of nature, the struggles of common people, and the challenges of modern life. He was also deeply influenced by the teachings of the great Indian philosopher, Sri Narayana Guru, and his works reflect his spiritual beliefs and quest for enlightenment. Asan was the poet of love. Asan was awarded with the title 'Maha Kavi" (Great Poet) in the year 1922 by Madras University considering his great works.

One of the Master piece work of Asan is the Poem 'Veena Poovu' which means 'Fallen Flower'. This poem stems from the depression of the poet when he saw a beautiful flower falling on the floor.

"Ha Pushpame Adhikathunga Padathilethra
Sobhichirunnithoru Rajni kanakkaye nee
Sree Bhoovil Asthira Asamshayam Innu ninte
Aa bhoothiyengu punarengu kidappithorthal"

The Poet is asking "Ha! flower, high among the boughs, you must have reigned once like a queen; Now look at your pitiable state; truly all happiness is transient". Asan raises many philosophical questions in this poem. Poet says the state of the fallen flower is the final fate of all human beings. There is nothing to do with the tears since we all have to accept the final destiny and truth.

Whole life of human on earth is nothing but equal to a beautiful dream and the death is nothing but an awakening from the deep sleep which is the ultimate truth. Poet also taught that suffering from grief is self-torture and ignorance. This poem can be deemed as a measuring scale of entire poems of Asan.

He was a poet who had cleansed the paths of old poetry tradition by sprinkling with the holy water of romantism and philosophy. Each of his poems are honey drops in the hearts of the readers. He fought through his poems against the then existing system. He observed that one must change himself or else the change will change everything. His poems are collection of colors filled with renaissance thoughts. He firmly believed that discrimination based on caste and religion are a hindrance to human progress.

Asan became Mahakavi without writing any Mahakavyas. He recognized the extraordinary scope and greatness of poetic art. The towering mountain peaks, the high-rolling ocean, the blooming forest land, the constellations and the solar system are all enriched by the poetic touch. Asan was a wake-up call in Modern Malayalam poetry. He evaluates life on the basis of Indian philosophy and modern humanistic philosophy. He never wrote a single poem to pass the time.

'Nalini', which describes the story of divine love, 'Veenapoov' which described the birth, infancy, childhood, youth, love affairs and death of a flower step by step, 'Leela', adopted the story of Lailamajnu, 'Chinthavishtayaya Seetha' which is guiding through the thoughts of forsaken Sita Devi, 'Duravastha' and Chandala Bhikshuki' questioning the caste discrimination, 'Karuna', 'Pookkalam' etc. are his important works. While the heroine in 'Duravastha' belongs to a high caste, in Chandalabhikshuki the heroine belongs to a lower caste. The aim of both the poems was nothing but to demolish the stronghold of casteism existed in the then society.

Kumaran Asan's impact on Malayalam literature and culture was enormous. He was a leading figure of the Kerala Renaissance, a movement that aimed to promote education, social reform, and cultural revival in the state. His works helped to create a new literary tradition in Malayalam, characterized by its modernism, humanism, and social awareness.

Asan was also a social activist and worked tirelessly for the upliftment of the poor and marginalized sections of society. He was a strong advocate for the importance of education in empowering individuals and communities, and he believed that literature and art had the power to transform society.

All the poems of Asan have the enlightenment that the medicinal value of sorrow itself can lead life from all sorrows to goodness. Asan believed that slavery is more dangerous than death. Foundation of freedom consciousness reflects in his poem was universal love and desire for transformation.

He became the flag bearer of human renaissance of the 20th century with the beauty of language, great imaginations and humanistic ideals. Shades of kindness, mercy and beyond that morality seen in all the poems make his poems beautiful and unforgettable. Kumaranasa, the poetic epic of Malayalam, was stolen by a boat accident occurred in Pallana River on 16th January, 1924.

Asan can be considered as the 'age maker' for the Malayalam language and modern Kerala. Being a visionary poet and social reformer who used his art to promote social and cultural change in Kerala, his poems will continue to inspire the generations of all age.

ꕥ

"Indian poetry and literature are not just words on a page, but a living, breathing reflection of the human experience, spanning generations and transcending borders."

ꕥ

XIV

Da Ra Bendre - Greatest Poet in the history of Kannada Literature

Dattatreya Ramachandra Bendre (*commonly known as Da Ra Bendre*) was one of the well famous poet of the Navodaya period who wrote in Kannada, a South Indian Dravidian language. He was born in Dharwad in Karnataka on 31st January 1896. Dattatreya used to write his poems in a pen name Ambikatanayadatta which means that Datta the son of Ambika. He was praised as "Varakavi" means "gifted poet". He was the second person among the eight recipients of Jnanapith Award for Kanndada, the highest literary honour conferred in India. He was also honoured with the time "Kannada Kula Tilaka". He was conferred Padma Shri by the Government of India.

In one of his poem 'Bendre wrote;

"The Eastern house shone with pearl-water
Gilded smoothly all over:
Flooding through the open doors
Light drenched the entire earth."

A study of the poetic life of Bendre proves that he used the spoken language of common people in his poems and that is the main reason for his success and leads to the wide acceptance of his poem among the people. The usage of colloquial words of Kannada language is one of the main beauty and attraction of Bendre's poems.

During 1922 Bendre formed Geleyara Gumbu (group of friends) with a main object as a peer group for promotion and learning of culture and literature. This group contains a large number of poets, intellectuals and writers of all parts of Karnataka State. Later during 1926 Bandre started a cultural movement Nada-habba, which is the celebration of the land and its culture. This festival is still being celebrated in Karnataka during Navarathri.

Though in the initial period Bendre started with simple and earthly romantic poetry, however later his works turned to socio and philosophical matters. Amongst his poetry collections, *'Nada Leela'* (The Play of Sounds) is the most remarkable one. He used the elements like patriotism, culture, mystical faith etc suitably in his poems. He used classical, spiritual, traditional and colloquial style in his poems. Symbolism is characteristic of his poetry. In almost all of his peoms a hidden layer of meaning can be found by a deep leader which proves his wisdom and command over language and literature.

'Naku Tanti' is one of the celebrated and complex poem wrote by Bendre. Naku Tanti means Four Strings. It mainly discusses the life to be four strings i.e male, female, offspring and nature. The four words used in this poem are *'Naanu', 'Neenu', 'Aanu' and 'Taanu'* which respectively means that husband, wife, offspring and nature. Naku Tanti revolves amongst these four elements. The poet explains the human life which revolves around these four strings. It is a poem of the human life stages from life to death.

Uyyale, Gangavataranaa, Krishna Kumari, Gari, Moorthi mattu Kamakastoori, Sooryapana, Nadaleele, Jeevalahari, Aralu Maralu, Namana, Sanchaya Uttarayana, Yaksha Yakshi, Baa Hataara, Idu Nabovani, Vinaya Olave Namma Badaku, Paraki, Chaitanyada puje, Budha, Kuniyonu Baa etc are his notable poetry collections. In the book 'Nada Lila' projects patriotism, reformation, traditions, Indian culture etc. Different symbolisms and idioms were brought by him in his poems like Patargiri.

His poems broken the concepts of conventional and orthodox poetrys. He was mainly focussing on folklore style of language in his poems which leads a great contribution to the Kannada Language. It is also relevant to point out that he was imprisoned for his book 'Nara Bali' (human sacrifice). Charging the offence of sedition he was house arrested following this book.

Many of his poems were used in Kannada Films. *'Innu Yaka barabillava', 'gama gama gamadasthava', 'mugila marige raga ratiya', 'Uttara druvadim Dakshina", "ilibu baa tayi", "moodala maneya"*etc. are examples of such songs.

Bendre enriched the Kannada literature for about eight decades with his heart-touching poetic style. He was a visionary poet whose works continue to inspire and enlighten readers to this day. His emphasis on usage of spoken language make him a figure of great importance not just in Kannada literature but in Indian culture as a whole. His legacy serves as a reminder of the power of literature to bring about positive change and inspire us to strive for a better world.

ꕥ

"The only way to rise in life is by acquiring knowledge, not by carrying the weight of gold."

ꕥ

XV

Changambuzha Krishna Pillai - Gandharva Kavi of Malayalam

Changampuzha Krishna Pillai was a miraculous poet in the history of Malayalam poetry. He is a poet who has magically changed the fantasy of an era. There is no generation in Kerala that does not know at least two lines of Changampuzha.

Changambuzha was born on October 10, 1911, in Edappally, near Kochi. He spent his early childhood in the serene surroundings of the countryside and developed a deep love for nature and its beauty. He was also fascinated by the stories and folk songs of his native land, which would later influence his writing.

Changampuzha's literary career began when he was a student, and he published his first poem at the age of 16. His early works were inspired by the romanticism of the English poets, and he often wrote about love and the beauty of nature.

He has acquired the richness of musicality from the tradition of the folk songs. Changampuzha, has been described as the poet of eternal youth. People used to call him the *'Ganagandharva of Malayalam'* and also the *'Orpheus of Malayalam'*. In fact he broke away the traditional themes of Malayalam Poetry and introduced a new style.

In a poem he wrote;

"Kapadamee Lokathil Athmarthamayoru
Hridayamundayathaanen parajayam"

In a world of hypocrisy, having a sincere heart was my failure. He loves the life very much. In another poem he wrote *"Enthu Vannalumenikkaswadikkanam, Munthiricharu polulloree jeevitham"*, *'What ever obstacles may come, but I want to celebrate this life like wine'.*

Ramanan, Vazhakkula, Yavanika, Spandikkunna Astimadam, Divya Geetham, Padunn Pishach, Aparadhikal, Neerunna Theechoola, Amritavichikal, Rakthapushpangal, Asthiyude Pookkal, Akashaganga, Aradhakar, Udyana Lakshmi Onappookkal, Kalakeli, Kelola Mala, Ch ooda Mani, Thalirthothukal, Thilothama , Devayani, Madirolsavam, Smashanathile Thulasi, Swara Ragasudha, Sreethilakam, Hemantha Chandrika, Padunna Pishach etc are the main works of Changabuzha.

Changampuzha's most famous work is the epic poem "Ramanan," which tells the story of the tragic love affair between Ramanan, a young man from a lower caste, and Clara, an upper-caste woman. The poem is a powerful critique of the social hierarchy prevalent in Kerala society at the time and the tragic consequences of forbidden love. "Ramanan" is widely regarded as a masterpiece of Malayalam literature and has been translated into many languages.

Another notable work by Changampuzha is "Karutha Pournami," a collection of poems that explores the themes of love and nature. The poems in this collection are characterized by their simplicity and lyrical beauty and have become some of the most popular poems in the Malayalam language.

Changampuzha's impact on Malayalam literature has been immense. His works have inspired generations of poets and writers, and his themes and style have become an integral part of the Malayalam literary tradition. His use of colloquial language and the depiction of rural life in his writing helped to popularize the language and make it more accessible to a wider audience. He is also credited with popularizing the use of the Malayalam language in contemporary literature.

Changampuzha's lyrics continue to influence Malayalam literature and culture. His emphasis on simplicity, emotional depth, and the power of regional dialects and colloquialisms have become important features of contemporary Malayalam poetry. He also emphasized the importance of social justice and equality, and his works continue to inspire social and cultural movements in Kerala.

Changambuzha believes that folklore was an integral part of Kerala's culture, and it was essential to preserve them for future generations. Accordingly he brought the beauty of folklore in his poems. He was a gifted poet and his poems are known for its romantic and lyrical style.

Changampuzha's poetry is known for its simplicity and lyrical beauty. He often used the traditional Malayalam meter and rhyme schemes in his poems. His works are characterized by their emotional depth and the power of their imagery, and they explore universal themes such as love, loss, and human emotions. His use of regional dialects and colloquialisms in his writing also contributed to the popularity of his works.

Youths of an Era treated the poems of Changambuzha as the expression of their own feelings. Even though the philosophical level may have dimmed in his poems, the melancholy picturised by Changampuzha belonged to that generation. The feeling conveyed by Changampuzha's poems are touchable the heart deeply in an indescribable manner. The main attraction of his poems are the language that flows from heart to heart. His poems made a generation cry as well as think. He built the magical kingdom of poetry with simple words of common men.

Changambuzha's works had a significant impact on the literary and cultural landscape of Kerala. His poems were widely read and enjoyed by people from all walks of life. He was known for his ability to connect with his readers and convey complex ideas in a simple and accessible manner. His works continue to be popular and are regularly taught in schools and colleges in Kerala.

Changambuzha's life and works are a testament to the power of literature to inspire social change and promote cultural heritage. He was a visionary poet who was able to bridge the gap between tradition and modernity and connect with his readers on a deep and emotional level. His sweat poetry continues to mesmerise the minds and souls of his readers.

℘

"The only true wisdom is in knowing you know nothing."

℘

XVI

P. Kunhiraman Nair - Poet Who is fond of Natural Beauty of Kerala

Mahakavi Panayanthatta Kunhiraman Nair, a celebrated Indian poet of Malayalam language who invokes romanticism and natural beauty of Kerala in his poems. He was affectionately known as Mahakavi P. His works not only depicted the essence of his surroundings but also reflected the socio-political realities of his era. His poety is the epitome of Keralaness which includes the greenery of Kerala, rituals, temples, deity concepts and so on.

Born on January 5, 1906, in Bellikoth, a village near Kanhangad in the Kasaragod district of Kerala, as son of Puravankara Kunjambu Nair, a physician, scholar of Sanskrit, and a vedantin, and Panayanthatta Kunjamma Amma. Kunhiraman Nair received his early education at a local primary school and with traditional teachers. Later, he went on to study Sanskrit at Punnassery Nambi Neelakanda Sharma's school in Pattambi, where he was reportedly a lazy student.

Despite his lack of interest in academics, Kunhiraman Nair's passion for writing and poetry was evident from his young age. His love for nature and the beauty of his homeland transformed him as poet of nature and symbolism. His poetry was not only aesthetically pleasing but also carried a deep message that resonated with his readers.

In the poem *'Soundarya Devatha"*, Kunhiraman Nair wrote;

"Athramel prananum prananay ninnu nee
Yathra Parayathe poyathuchithamo?
Vinnil Velichamezhuthi Ninneedumo
Kannil Our Kurikoode Kshana Prabhe?"
"After you have become the soul of my soul,
Is it appropriate to leave without saying any words..?

Can you write the light of the sky?
Once again in the eyes, my shining beloved!"

The lyrics that depict the broken hearts in love. Kunhiraman Nair was the calm flow of the ocean of sweetness; the great beauty of the word that has flowed into Malayalam. It was a birth only for poetry.

Mahakavi P's contribution to Malayalam literature are testament to the power of language and the beauty of nature, and great works he donated to Indian literature will never be forgotten.

P. Kunhiraman Nair was a literary genius who lived a nomadic lifestyle, traveling across Kerala and immersing himself in different cultures. His literary works encompassed various genres, including poetry, novels, short stories etc. He was recognized with numerous awards and accolades for his contribution to Malayalam literature, which includes the prestigious Kerala Sahitya Academy Award for Poetry and the Kendra Sahitya Academy Award. Nileswaram Raja honoured him by giving the title Bhakthakavi. Similarly Raja of Cochin honoured him by awarding the title of Sahitya Nipunan.

Mahakavi P's literary journey began with spiritual poems, but his work took a new direction with the publication of Nirapara in 1944. Some of his well-known poetry include *Kaliyachan, Onassadya, Pookalam, Vasantholsavam, Karpoora Mazha, Neeranjanam, Prapanjam, Thamarathoni, Vayalkarayil, Ratholsavam, Koduthu Mudinja Mavu, Neeranjanam, Soundarya Devatha, Balamrutham, Anthithiri, Nakshathramaala, Bhadradeepam* etc. He also wrote Short stories and novels including *Parayi Petta Panthirukulam, Udayaragam, Vichara Vicharam, Mekhamala etc.*

Kunhiraman Nair's autobiography, *Kaviyude Kaalpaadukal (The Footprints of a Poet)*, is a celebrated prose work in Malayalam which is a testament to his life and literary achievements, which continue to inspire and captivate readers to this generation. His other works like *Enne Thirayunna Njan, Nityakanyakaye Thedi* etc are also celebrated works.

Even after years of his departure, Mahakavi P. remains a revered figure in Kerala, with several memorials and institutions dedicated to his life and works. His lyrics continues to inspire and captivate readers to this day. Mahakavi P.'s legacy is a testament to his exceptional talent and dedication to the art of literature. His contributions have left an indelible mark on the literary landscape of Kerala.

He is a literary icon who has left an indelible mark in the literary horizon. His exceptional talent has enabled him to capture the beauty of the world around him and enrich the culture of the motherland.

Mahakavi P. will always remain as a shining star in the Malayalam literature as he was. His departure marked the completion of a poetic life of pure love for nature and beauty. Mahakavi Akkitham, another famous poet in Malayalam marked Mahakavi P with the following words in his poem;

"Who born in Kanhangad
As a Poet from feet to hair
Who drowned till his midlife
In the beautiful Perar River
He is none other than Kunhiraman Nair
A greatman who amazes the World"

Mahakavi P. Kunhiraman Nair, who passed away in 1978, remains as an eternal spring in Malayalam poetry.

ꙮ

"The world is a beautiful book, but of little use to him who cannot read it."

ꙮ

XVII

Vayalar Rama Varma - The Revelutionary Poet of Kerala

"Njan Ente Vathmeekathil
Ithiri neram dhyana Leelanayirunnath
Maunamaay Maranalla
Maunathe Maha sabdamakkuvaan
Nishchanchala dhyaanathe
Chalanamaay shakthiyaay Unarthuvaan"

"I was in deep meditation in my termite mound for a while, not to become silent, but to turn the silence to loud voice; to awaken unmoving meditation into moving power". The above lines of power were generated from the heart of a Malayalam poet and he is Vayalar Rama Varma, the evergreen Malayalam Poet.

Vayalar Rama Varma, was Born in 1928 in the village Vayalar of Alappuzha District, Kerala as the son of Vellarappalli Kerala Varma and Vayalar Raghavapparambil Ambalika Thamburatti. His poetic journey began at a young age. Later Rama Varma came to be known by the name of his native Vayalar. His poems were the reflection of the socio-political issues of his time, and he fearlessly voiced his opinions through his lyrics. His poems are the flowers that bloom, drawing in the warmth, beauty and beauty of the soil. He was known as the popular revolutionary poet of Kerala.

Vayalar is one of the few geniuses who are poet by birth. He is known as the Gandharva of Malayalam poetry. Apart from being a poet, he is more famous as a film lyricist. He composed thousands of songs for Malayalam film industry and his lyrics captured the joys and sorrows of the common men of the society. Vayalar is a poet who brought music into the soul of poetry and invoked poetry into the heart of songs. He has conquered the musical universe by about 2,000 songs written by him, perhaps unsurpassed by anyone else.

Vayalar is a poet who can claim the tradition of Jayadeva Kavi. Vayalar had a deep knowledge of Indian cultures and Vedic epics and his lyrics are imbued with the vibrancy of the Indian ancient culture. He had also adapted Puranas and mythological characters in his own style in his poems. 'Tadaka', 'Ravanaputhri' etc are examples of such poems.

His first poetry collection was *'Padamudrakal'*. The pain of the partition of India reflects in this poem. He wrote in that poem :

"Karayunnille ningal
India than Karal vetti
Kuruthikkalam Theertha
Kannerin katha kelkke"

The translation is that *"Don't you cry while hearing the story of creation of killing field by cut out the liver of India'.*

*Konthayum Poonoolum, Enikku Maranamilla, Mulankad, Thadaka, Ravanaputhri, Ente Mattolikkavithakal, Aswamedham, Ayisha*etc. are his other important works. In 1957, during the EMS government, the song "*Bali kuteerangale*", which was written for the opening ceremony of the Palayam Raktasakshi Mandapam, was a huge hit.

What was lost in poetry later became an asset to Malayalam film songs when Vayalar established himself in the film song area. He wrote so many songs on the canvas of time which survives for ever. Vayalar's son Sharath Chandra Varma is also a prolific lyricist in the Malayalam film music industry.

Vayalar's poems will bring the readers to the heights of philosophy and make them to sit and meditate. His lyrics provide a new vision for human life. His poems and songs always remind us that God takes form in the human mind as goodness and love. He makes it clear in his poems that the human willpower cannot be conquered even if they are locked in jail. He always reminds us through his poetry that there is nothing greater than humanity and love.

Vayalar's literary contributions were not only significant but also revolutionary. His works were a reflection of his beliefs and ideologies, which evolved over time. His shift towards communism was a testament to his commitment to social justice and equality. He used his platform to challenge the status quo and bring about change in society.

His popularity as a poet was unparalleled, and he was known for bringing poetry to the common man's domain. His works were widely read and appreciated, and he was considered a literary giant of his time. His writing style was unique, and he had a way of capturing the essence of life in his poetry. His works were a reflection of his deep understanding of human emotions and his ability to express them in a way that resonated with his readers.

Vayalar worked with the communist movement and progressive cultural and literary movements in Kerala. His anti-China speech turned as a topic of discussion amongst the communist movements in Kerala and it also invites high criticism. He has the courage to look at the sky sat beneath his own principles. His lyrics called upon the generations to raise the pen as sword to eradicate inequalities in the society for the sake of great humanity.

Human transformation through scientific evolution is the principle which rooted in his poems. The reader can experience the horseshoes of scientific progress in his poetry. 'Enikku Maranamilla', 'Galileo','Chalanam Chalanam' etc. are examples of such poems.

Despite much criticism, he shone like a star in the sky. Even today his lyrics are being celebrated by the readers in their loneliness, frenzy and bliss. Vayalar's poetic tradition will be remembered as long as the language Malayalam exists.

"The uniqueness of poetry lies in the fact that it can communicate the most complex ideas with the simplest words."

XVIII

Mahakavi Kanhaiyalal Sethia - The Poet of Rajasthan's Soul

Mahakavi Kanhaiyalal Sethia, also known as Kanhaiyalal Sethia, was a prominent Indian poet, lyricist, and playwright from Rajasthan. He was one of the most celebrated poets of the 20th century in Hindi literature. His works are known for their simplicity, emotional depth, and the ability to capture the essence of Rajasthan's culture and soul. After completing his education, he started working as a teacher in various schools in Rajasthan. He also worked as an editor for several Hindi newspapers and magazines.

His first poem was published when he was only 14 years old. Despite facing several challenges, Sethia continued to write and publish his works, which soon gained popularity and made him a well-known figure in the literary circles of Rajasthan.

Sethia's poetry is deeply rooted in the culture, traditions, and folklore of Rajasthan. He drew inspiration from the vibrant and colorful life of the people of Rajasthan and captured their joys, sorrows, and struggles in his works. His poems are marked by their simplicity, clarity of expression, and the ability to connect with readers at a personal level. His themes range from love, life, and spirituality to social issues, including poverty, injustice, and inequality.

"Yuddh Nahin Hai Naash Maatra Hi,
Yuddh Svayam Nirmaata Hai,
Ladaa Na Jisne Yuddh Rashtr Vah,
Kachcha Hi Rah Jaata Hai,
Nahin Tilak Ke Yogya Sheesh Vah,
Jis Par Hua Prahaar Nahin,
Rahee Kunwaari Mutthi Vah Jo,
Pakad Sakkee Talavaar Nahin."

It reflects the principle of Sethia. Meaning of the above line is "*War is only destruction, war creates itself; One who did not fight for the nation remains immature; No head is worthy of a crown which has not faced an attack; And the fist which couldn't grasp the sword remains a virgin.*" Sethia conveyed the message that war should be avoided as it only brings destruction, and those who do not defend their nation remain weak and immature. It emphasizes the importance of courage and the readiness to defend oneself against attacks.

In Hindi, he authored 18 books, including Vanphool , Agniveena, Mera Yug , Deepkiran, Pratibimb, Aaj Himalaya Bola, Khuli Krirkiyan Chaure Raaste, Pranam, Marm, Anam, Nirgranth, Swagat, Deh Videh, Akask Ganga, Vaaman - Viraat, Nishpatti, Shreyas, Trayee. He also wrote 14 books in Rajasthani and two in Urdu i.e Taj Mahal and Gulchi.

Kanhaiyalal's Rajasthani poetry is particularly noteworthy. Two of his poems have achieved cult status and international recognition. "Dharti Dhoran Ri" is considered the official anthem of Rajasthan. The renowned filmmaker Gautam Ghosh has created a documentary called Land of the Sand Dunes based on this poem, which received the Swarna Kamal (Golden Lotus) award from the Indian government.

One of the most remarkable aspects of Sethia's poetry is its ability to transcend the boundaries of language, region, and culture. His works have a universal appeal and can be enjoyed by people of all ages and backgrounds. His message of love, compassion, and social justice has touched the hearts of millions of readers and has inspired generations of poets and writers.

Sethia's impact on Hindi literature and Rajasthan's culture cannot be overstated. He was a pioneer of the modern Hindi poetry movement and was instrumental in bringing about a renaissance in

Rajasthani literature. His works have been the subject of numerous academic studies and literary analyses, and he has been awarded several prestigious literary awards for his contributions to Hindi literature.

Apart from his literary contributions, Kanhaiyalal Sethia was also known for his philanthropic work. He was a staunch believer in social justice and worked towards the upliftment of the underprivileged sections of society. He established the "Kanhaiya Lal Sethia Foundation" to support various social and cultural causes.

Kanhaiyalal Sethia received several prestigious awards throughout his career as a writer. He was honored with the Sahitya Akademi Award for his work in Lilatansa. In 1986, he was awarded the Jnanapitha Moortidevi Award, and in 1987, he received the Suryamal Mishran Shikhar Award.

In 2004, Kanhaiyalal was conferred with the Padma Shri award. He also received the Sahithya Vascahpati by the Hindi Sahitya Sammelan, Prayag, and the Sahitya Manishi by the Sahitya Academy, Udaipur.

Kanhaiyalal Sethia's impact on Hindi literature is significant. He was a prominent figure in the Hindi literary world and was widely regarded as one of the most accomplished poets of his time. His poetry has been translated into several languages, including English, and has been published in many literary journals and magazines. He was awarded the Sahitya Akademi Award in 1968 for his contribution to Hindi literature.

The Rajasthan Sahitya Akademi also awarded him the prestigious "Mahakavi" title in recognition of his literary achievements. Sethia's legacy is a testament to the power of literature to bring about positive change in society and to transcend the boundaries of language, region, and culture.

ဆ

"My eyes become restless when I see the beauty of the beloved. And my heart, like a horse, is tied to the reins of love.

ဆ

XIX

Nissim Ezekiel - The Jewish Poet from India

Nissim Ezekiel was a multi-talented Indian Jewish Poet who was born on 16th December 1924 in Bombay Presidency of British India. His contribution to Indian English poetry should always be remembered. He died in the year 2004 at the age of 74. In his poem *'Paradise"* he wrote;

"But when the differences arose
On how to cross a desert patch,
We lost a friend whose stylish prose
Was quite the best of all our batch
A shadow falls on us and grows"

He was not only a renowned poet but also an actor, playwright, editor, and art critic. Ezekiel played a pivotal role in shaping the literary landscape of postcolonial India, particularly in the realm of Indian Poetry in English. He was a leading figure in the Indian literary scene of the 1950s and 1960s and was one of the pioneers of modern Indian poetry in English. His works explore themes of identity, religion, culture, and colonialism, and his unique style and voice have had a lasting impact on Indian poetry.

This experience of traveling across the world and working in diverse roles would influence his writing and broaden his perspective on life. Despite the challenges, Ezekiel persevered and continued to write and publish his works, becoming one of the most prominent voices in Indian English poetry.

Ezekiel's poetry is known for its humour, irony, and social commentary. He often wrote about the struggles of ordinary people and their lives in post-colonial India. His poems are also infused with a sense of his Jewish identity and the history of the Jewish people. His early works, such as "A Time to Change" (1952) and "Sixty Poems" (1953), established him as a leading voice in Indian poetry in English.

Ezekiel's poetry was a reflection of his experiences as an Indian Jew, and his writing often explored themes of identity, culture, and tradition. Search for own identity was always a theme in Ezekiel's poems. He wrote about himself that "A *mugging Jew among the wolves; They told me that I had killed the Christ.*" His strong feelings of search of owns identity reflects in this lines. In his poem "Patriot", he protested against the radicalism and violence amongst the people of our nation.

One of Ezekiel's most famous works is his collection of poems titled "The Unfinished Man" (1960). The collection explores themes of alienation, identity, and modernity, and is considered a landmark in Indian poetry. The title poem, "The Unfinished Man," is a meditation on the nature of the self and the human condition. The poem's narrator reflects on his life and the many things he has left unfinished, suggesting that the human experience is always incomplete.

Ezekiel's other notable works include "Hymns in Darkness" (1976), "Latter-Day Psalms" (1982), and "Collected Poems" (1989). His poetry is characterized by a distinctively Indian voice and a blend of Western and Indian literary traditions.

In the poem "The Truth about the floods", he gave a realist picture of the lack of proper disaster management in a flood affected area.

Ezekiel's impact on Indian literature is significant. He was one of the Indian poets who helped to establish the Indian English literary tradition. He also influenced a generation of Indian poets and writers who followed in his footsteps. His unique voice and style continue to inspire and challenge readers and writers in India and around the world.

Some of his poetry leads to philosophical thoughts. He was a poet of sincerity and integrity and he concentrates in the religion of love and charity. He was a distinguished scholar.

In addition to his literary contributions, Ezekiel was also a noted educator and cultural commentator. He taught at several colleges and universities in India and was a founding member of the Writers' Workshop in Calcutta. He was also involved in promoting the arts and culture in India, serving as the chairman of the Indian Council for Cultural Relations and the Sahitya Academy.

Ezekiel's writings reflect his commitment to social justice, secularism, and the importance of cultural diversity. He believed that literature had the power to bridge cultural and religious divides and to promote understanding and empathy. His poetry, plays, and essays are a testament to his belief in the transformative power of literature and the arts.

In 1983, Ezekiel was honoured with the Sahitya Academy Award for his collection, Latter-Day Psalms, by the Sahitya Academy, India's National Academy of Letters. His writing style has been praised for its subtle, restrained, and well-crafted diction, which deals with common and mundane themes in a manner that showcases both cognitive profundity and an unsentimental, realistic sensibility. This approach has had a significant impact on the trajectory of Indian English poetry.

Ezekiel's modernist innovations and techniques have enriched and established Indian English language poetry, expanding its scope beyond purely spiritual and orientalist themes to encompass a broader range of concerns and interests. These include familial events, individual angst, and sceptical societal introspection. His contributions have been instrumental in moving Indian English literature forward and elevating it to new heights.

Nissim Ezekiel was a true visionary who left an indelible mark on Indian literature and the arts. His legacy continues to inspire and influence artists and writers around the world. Nissim Ezekiel was a pioneering poet, playwright, and literary critic who made a significant contribution to Indian literature in English. His unique voice and style, as well as his commitment to social justice and cultural diversity, have had a lasting impact on Indian poetry and culture. He remains an important figure in Indian literary history and his works continue to inspire and challenge readers and writers around the world.

ꙮ

"The woman is the light of the home, the lamp of the nation, the hope of the world."

ꙮ

XX

Kamala Surayya - The Royal Fragrance of Indian Poetry

Madhavikutty alias Kamala Das was a writer who has proven to be equally proficient in Malayalam and English literature. Later, when she converted to Islam, she adopted the name Kamala Surayya. She proved proficiency in Writing Novels and stories in Malayalam and poetry in English. Born on March 31, 1934, in Kerala, she is considered one of the most iconic poets of the Indian English poetry. Her works focused on themes of love, sexuality, and the inner struggles of women, and her writing style was characterized by its raw honesty and vivid imagery.

With her unique style and powerful voice, Kamala Surayya left an indelible mark on the literary world. Despite facing criticism and controversy for her bold and unconventional writing, Kamala Surayya remained steadfast in her commitment to artistic expression. Her legacy as a trailblazing writer and feminist icon endures to this day.

Kamala Suraiyya began her literary career at a young age, publishing her first collection of poems, '*Summer in Calcutta*'. Other important poems written by her are *The Descendants, Old Play House and Other Poems, Only the Soul know how to Sing, The Sirens, An Introduction, Tonight this Savage Rite, The Anamalai Poems* etc. Alphabet of Lust is a Novel wrote by her in English. *Manasi, Manomi, Chandanamarangal, Kadal Mayooram, Amavasi, Kavadam, Vandikkalakal* etc. are some of the Novels written in Malayalam. *Ente Katha, Neermathalam Poothakalam, Balyam Ente Nashta Vasthram, Balyakala Smaranakal, Vishadam Pookkunna Marangal* etc. are her Memories. Her autobiography, *"My Story,"* caused a stir in conservative Indian society for its frank discussions of female sexuality and her own personal experiences. Kamala Suraiyya continued to publish poetry, fiction, and essays throughout her life, becoming a prolific and influential writer in Indian literature.

Her English Poems are the ultimate form of 'Indianization of English Language. The poem *'An Introduction'* begins with the following lines;

"I don't know politics but I know the names
Of those in power, and can repeat them like
Days of week, or names of months, beginning with Nehru.
I am Indian, very brown, born in Malabar,
I speak three languages, write in
Two, dream in one.
Don't write in English, they said, English is
Not your mother-tongue. Why not leave
Me alone, critics, friends, visiting cousins,
Every one of you? Why not let me speak in
Any language I like? The language I speak,
Becomes mine, its distortions, its queernesses
All mine, mine alone."

The life of a woman who lives in a patriarchal society is beautifully picturised in the above poem. Poetess also describes the jealous nature of her friends and relatives who cannot endure her skills. Kamala also declares that the language in which she writes with all its imperfections are her own language. A self-respecting poet who is proud of her talent can be read in this poem.

Kamala Suraiyya's poetry is known for its raw emotional power and sensual imagery. Her poems often explore the complexities of love and relationships, both within and outside of marriage. She frequently addressed the struggles and desires of women, and her work is considered to be a seminal contribution to feminist literature in India. Her writing style is characterized by its honesty and directness, with a focus on the inner world of the individual.

She believed that writing is a self-sacrifice. One who goes through her poems and other writings can find that she was actually searching for love for the whole of her life. A passion to conquer anything in the intensity of love is the speciality of her writings. She has written her writings by mixing life and imagination. Her writings were her breathing air.

Kamala Suraiyya's impact on Indian literature and society was significant. Her work challenged traditional ideas of gender and sexuality, and her frank discussions of personal experience paved the way for other writers to explore these topics in their own work. She was a vocal advocate for women's rights and was known for her activism on behalf of marginalized communities. Her poetry and prose continue to inspire readers and writers, and her legacy as a feminist icon endures to this day.

Kamala Suraiyya's work teaches us the importance of honesty and vulnerability in writing. Her poetry is a powerful testament to the inner life of the individual, and her frank discussions of sexuality and personal experience paved the way for other writers to explore these topics in their own work. Her advocacy for women's rights and marginalized communities is an example of the power of literature to effect change in society.

Kamala Surayya is being read again and again which proves that her writings are eternally young. She was a pioneering figure in Indian literature, known for her raw and honest depictions of love, sexuality, and the inner struggles of women. Her work continues to inspire readers and writers alike, and her legacy as a feminist icon endures to this day. Through her writing, she challenged traditional ideas of gender and sexuality, and her advocacy for marginalized communities serves as a powerful reminder of the role that literature can play in effecting social change.

"Love is not a feeling, It's an art, like poetry."

Citation And Reference

This book has been written by referencing various books of the poets referred in this book, websites, including Wikipedia, in order to gather valuable information and data about the legend poets. The author has taken care to ensure that all information presented is accurate and properly cited to give credit to the sources.

Although every effort has been made to ensure the accuracy and completeness of the information presented in this book, human errors may still occur. If any reader discovers any errors in this book, I respectfully welcome their feedback and encourage them to bring it to my attention. Such feedback is valuable to me, and I will take all necessary steps to correct any errors and improve the content of this book in future editions. Thank you for your understanding and support.

9 798890 026286

Printed by Libri Plureos GmbH in Hamburg, Germany